The New Hampshire Colony

Bob Italia
ABDO Publishing Company

visit us at
www.abdopub.com

Published by ABDO Publishing Company, 4940 Viking Drive, Suite 622, Edina, Minnesota 55435. Copyright © 2001 by Abdo Consulting Group, Inc. International copyrights reserved in all countries. No part of this book may be reproduced in any form without written permission from the publisher.

Printed in the United States.

Cover Photo Credit: North Wind Picture Archives
Interior Photo Credits: North Wind Picture Archives (pages 5, 7, 9, 11, 13, 15, 17, 19, 21, 23, 24, 25, 27, 29); Corbis (pages 18, 20, 22)

Contributing Editors: Tamara L. Britton, Kate A. Furlong, and Christine Fournier
Book Design and Graphics: Neil Klinepier

Library of Congress Cataloging-in-Publication Data

Italia, Bob, 1955-
  The New Hampshire Colony / Bob Italia.
    p. cm. -- (The colonies)
  Includes index.
  ISBN 1-57765-585-0
  1. New Hampshire--History--Colonial period, ca. 1600-1775--Juvenile
literature. I. Title II. Series

F37 .I83 2001
974.2'02--dc21

2001016120

Contents

New Hampshire

Native Americans first settled in New Hampshire. In 1614, explorer John Smith claimed New Hampshire's land for England. The first English colonists founded the Pannaway Plantation. The towns of Dover, Portsmouth (PORT-smuth), Exeter, and Hampton followed.

New Hampshire became a royal **province** in 1679. It was subject to England's laws. But the colony also created its own laws and government.

The New Hampshire colonists fished, traded furs, sold lumber, and farmed. They built their own homes and made their own clothes. Colonial children helped with chores.

The colonists fought many wars against the Native Americans and the French. After the wars ended in 1760, New Hampshire became very successful. Soon, the colonists wanted independence from England.

On January 5, 1776, New Hampshire adopted a state **constitution**. New Hampshire colonists fought in the American Revolution. New Hampshire became the ninth state in 1788.

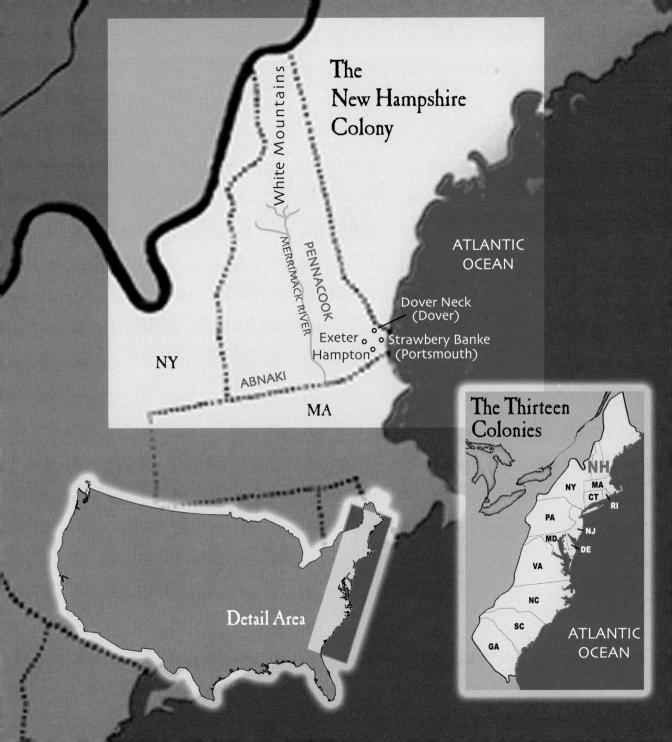

The New Hampshire Colony

White Mountains

MERRIMACK RIVER

PENNACOOK

ATLANTIC OCEAN

Dover Neck (Dover)

Exeter
Hampton

Strawbery Banke (Portsmouth)

NY

ABNAKI

MA

Detail Area

The Thirteen Colonies

NH

NY   MA
CT   RI
PA
MD   NJ
DE
VA

NC

SC

GA

ATLANTIC OCEAN

Early History

New Hampshire is a small state in northeastern North America. Most of the region is hilly. It also has mountains, woods, and lakes.

Before the English arrived, about 12,000 Native Americans lived in present-day New Hampshire. They were organized into clans, bands, and larger tribes. Most villages had less than 100 people. The Native Americans all spoke the **Algonquian** (al-GON-kwee-an) language. They controlled northeastern North America.

The most powerful tribe was the Pennacook (PEN-uh-kook). Many of their villages were along the Merrimack River. Another powerful tribe was the Abnaki (a-BEN-ah-kee). They lived in the west.

The Pennacook and Abnaki depended on hunting, fishing, and growing corn. They moved with the change of seasons to search for food. They built birchbark and dugout canoes to travel the rivers and lakes.

New Hampshire's White Mountains

The First Explorers

In 1603, Martin Pring arrived in present-day New Hampshire. He was the first European to explore the area. He was searching for a shortcut across America to India. He was also looking for sassafras trees. The English believed sassafras was a powerful medicine.

Samuel de Champlain was the second European to explore New Hampshire. He came in 1605 to explore the region for France. Champlain did not stay in New Hampshire. He went on to discover Lake Champlain. He also founded Quebec (kwuh-BEK) in Canada.

In 1614, John Smith came to New Hampshire. He had founded the Virginia Colony in 1607. Smith explored the land, made maps, and claimed the land for England. He reported his find to King James I. Smith named the land North Virginia. Later, King James renamed it New England.

Samuel de Champlain

Settlement

In 1620, England organized the Council for New England. It was to colonize present-day New England.

In 1621, the council gave land in New England to Sir Ferdinando Gorges (fer-de-NAN-do GOR-jez) and Captain John Mason. Mason and Gorges wanted to harvest the land's natural resources.

Mason sent David Thomson to settle near present-day Portsmouth in 1623. Thomson and the colonists called their settlement the Pannaway Plantation. They fished and traded with the Native Americans. But in 1630, Pannaway Plantation was abandoned.

Edward and William Hilton founded New Hampshire's first town in 1623. They chose a neck of land near the Pannaway Plantation. They named it Dover Neck, and later, Dover.

In 1629, Mason received a new, larger land grant. Mason came from Hampshire County in England. So he called this land New Hampshire.

In 1630, Captain Walter Neale sailed to North America. He landed near the Pannaway Plantation. At the time, wild strawberries covered the riverbanks. The colonists called their town Strawbery Banke. In 1653, the colonists renamed the town Portsmouth.

Reverend John Wheelwright settled Exeter in 1638. The next year, Hampton was established. In 1641, Massachusetts Bay Colony ruled these four settlements.

In 1679, New Hampshire left the rule of Massachusetts Bay Colony. In 1740, boundary disagreements with Massachusetts Bay Colony were settled. The next year, Benning Wentworth became New Hampshire's first royal governor.

Benning Wentworth

Government

At first, the Council for New England ruled New Hampshire. Then it was governed by the Massachusetts Bay Colony. Finally, in 1679, it became a royal **province**.

As a royal province, New Hampshire had a president and council appointed by England's royalty. By 1700, the men of the colony elected an assembly to represent them. The assembly met in Portsmouth.

New Hampshire was still subject to England's laws. But since England was across the ocean, it was difficult to govern the colonies. So each colony also created its own laws and government.

The colonists conducted business in meetinghouses. There, they made laws, formed government, and chose leaders. They also held various courts there.

The first meetinghouses were large, square buildings. These buildings were used for church services and town meetings. Each community also had a minister.

For years, New Hampshire followed Massachusetts Bay Colony's laws. According to these laws, crimes had strict punishments. Drunkenness or working on Sunday were lesser crimes. They were punished with public whippings, the **stocks**, or fines. Major offenses like murder and kidnapping were punishable by death.

An early New Hampshire meetinghouse

Life in the Colony

The early New Hampshire colonists learned to live on their own. They worked on the farm, in the woods, or at sea. They traded goods with each other. Cash was seldom used or seen.

Most women took care of their families. They cooked the meals. They preserved pumpkins, apples, beans, and other foods. They washed and sewed clothes. And they spun flax and wool.

Most New Hampshire farmers only grew what they needed. They did not need slaves to work their small farms. The African slave trade often brought slaves to Portsmouth. But few New Hampshire colonists bought slaves.

Travel was difficult for the colonists. When possible, colonists traveled by water. Where roads existed, people rode in coaches and wagons. Ice, snow, and mud often made roads too dangerous to travel.

New England colonists celebrated few holidays. Each Sunday, or Sabbath, the colonists went to church. On this day, they were not allowed to work or play games.

New England colonists did not celebrate Christmas. They did not celebrate any of the Church of England's holidays. In fact, people were fined for playing games on Christmas Day.

The first colonists did celebrate Thanksgiving. But it was not like today's Thanksgiving Day. Beginning in 1631, colonists held a harvest festival every few years. Their meal consisted of wild game, corn, squash, beans, and pumpkins. It became a regular holiday in 1676.

Colonists used sleighs to travel during the winter.

Making a Living

The New Hampshire colonists made a living by trading furs, selling lumber, fishing, and farming. Beaver skin was popular in Europe. Traders and trappers went deep into New Hampshire's forests to trap the animals.

Fishermen caught cod and pollock. The fish were split and salted aboard the fishing ships. Then they were stored under the ship's deck. Once ashore, the fish were spread on racks to dry. Some fish parts were used to make oil. And fish heads were used as hog food or **fertilizer**.

The forests were important to the colonists. The English Navy used the tall, white pines for ship masts. The colonists built ships in many of New Hampshire's coast towns. They also cut timber for homes.

New Hampshire's forests made farming difficult. Colonists cleared the land tree by tree. They removed each tree stump by hand, pulled it out by a team of oxen, or burned it. After all this work, New Hampshire farm fields were still littered with rocks and tree stumps.

Squash, pumpkins, beans, corn, and potatoes grew well in New Hampshire's fields. Apple and pear orchards also did well. Colonists planted flax to make linen for clothing.

Raising livestock was easier than growing crops. The colonists raised cattle, horses, sheep, and pigs.

The colonists built ships with New Hampshire's plentiful lumber.

Food

The early New Hampshire colonists hunted wild game in the forests. They also depended on the fish from the streams, rivers, and ocean.

Native Americans taught the colonists how to plant, raise, and prepare corn. Corn dishes like hominy, pone, samp, and succotash became part of their diet.

Colonists ground corn in a wooden **mortar** or a hollowed stone. They used a heavy wooden **pestle** to pound the corn. Hand mills soon replaced the mortar and pestle. Later, colonists used windmills and water mills.

Pumpkins were another important food. They grew easily even in the harshest land. Colonists kept pumpkins for long periods of time in deep, dry cellars. They used pumpkins to make bread and stews. They also ate pumpkins as a vegetable.

Other important crops included potatoes and beans. Colonists made sugar from maple tree sap.

A mortar and pestle

Colonists drank cider, made from the many apples in the orchards. Another popular drink was perry, made from pears. Dried beef and salt pork were popular meat products.

Colonists press apples to make cider.

Clothing

Most New Hampshire colonists made clothes out of linen or leather. But wealthy colonists bought fabrics like calico, flannel, silk, and velvet. These fabrics were brought on ships from England or the West Indies.

Wealthy women used these fabrics to make dresses or **bonnets**. They also wore **petticoats**, shawls, and silk hoods. Rich men wore breeches and jackets of finer fabrics as well. Rich men and women's clothes were dyed in bright colors.

Colonial farmers and craftsmen usually wore leather breeches and linen shirts. Their clothes were colored with brown and green dye. This helped them hunt in the forest. Their wives had skirts, aprons, and bonnets made of linen.

Linen was made from flax, a plant with silklike fibers. The colonists spun flax into thread on a spinning wheel. They wove the threads into fine white cloth on a hand loom. The cloth was made into sheets, towels, tablecloths, shirts, undergarments, and dresses.

A spinning wheel

Colonists also tanned their own leather. First, they washed the animal hides in a stream. Then they soaked them in several liquids to remove dirt and hair. To preserve the skins, the colonists soaked them in a bark and water mixture. Then they oiled the leather to prepare it for use. It was made into jackets, breeches, or shoes. This process took more than six months.

Many colonists wore hand-spun cloaks to church.

Homes

Most early colonial homes were log cabins. Colonists stuffed moss or clay in the spaces between the logs. The roof was made of bark, thatch, or split logs. There were few windows, and they had no glass panes. So colonists used shutters to keep out the wind and rain.

Most homes had a huge fireplace. Women cooked meals over the open fire. The fire also kept the cabin warm in the winter. And in the summer, the smoke kept the mosquitoes and black flies away.

Later, colonists built houses with wood frames covered in wooden planks. The wood frames were held together with wooden pegs. Other houses were made of brick.

Inside the home, plates, bowls, and spoons were also made of wood. Colonists split cattle horns to make drinking glasses. They made pots of iron and brass. Colonists used **tallow** and bayberry candles to light their homes.

Early colonists also built garrison houses. These homes protected them from Native American attacks. All of the neighbors built the garrison house. But only one family lived inside. In times of danger, everyone stayed at the garrison.

Garrison houses had a few small windows. They were covered with strong shutters. The door was often made of strong wood, such as oak.

Statesman Daniel Webster was born in this 1700s farmhouse in New Hampshire.

Children

When children were old enough, they helped with chores. They learned how to sew and make soap and candles. They picked berries and chopped flax. They hunted and worked in the fields.

Early colonial children attended a dame school. A woman held class in her house. Children usually attended dame school for two years. Then some went on to grammar school.

Colonial children learned the alphabet, reading skills, some prayers, and simple arithmetic. Some even learned how to write. They learned from a hornbook. It was a written lesson fastened to a wooden board. It was covered with a clear sheet made from horn.

When New Hampshire was ruled by Massachusetts Bay Colony, it was subject to its education laws. The Education Act of 1647 required someone to teach reading, writing,

A boy carrying his tops.

and arithmetic in every town of 50 families. Every town of 100 families had to have a grammar school. Grammar school prepared boys for college. Girls began to learn how to manage a household.

When they could, children liked to play games. Tag, hide-and-seek, and hopscotch were popular. In the winter, children went ice-skating.

Boys also liked to play marbles, fly kites, and spin tops. Girls liked to play with dolls carved from wood or made from cornhusks. They also liked to embroider.

A young girl brings the cattle home.

Native Americans

At first, New Hampshire colonists had little trouble with Native Americans. They lived together peacefully and traded goods.

But in time, the Native Americans grew distrustful of the colonists. The **Puritans** tried to subject them to English law, which they did not understand. They were cheated out of their lands. The Native Americans rebelled against the colonists. They fought King Philip's War in 1675.

The French also influenced the Native Americans. Both the French and the English wanted to claim land in America. The Native Americans sided with the French against the English. Soon, a series of battles erupted.

In 1689, King William's War was declared. Queen Anne's War began in 1702. And King George's War followed in 1744. **Raids** were common throughout these wars. Both sides suffered.

The battles ended with the French and Indian War. The war began in 1754, when the French built a fort on the

Ohio River. Many **raids** over land ownership took place. New Hampshire's Robert Rogers and John Stark became famous military leaders during the war.

Finally, in 1760, the French surrendered. The Native Americans moved north. All of New Hampshire was now open for colonial settlement.

Colonists attack Native Americans during King Philip's War.

The Road to Statehood

After the French and Indian War, towns began to spring up all over New Hampshire. More than 100 towns were built after 1761.

Governor Benning Wentworth died in 1770. His nephew, Sir John Wentworth, became the new governor. Sir John Wentworth built roads. He published a state map. He organized the state **militia** (muh-LISH-uh). And he helped start Dartmouth College.

During this time, England was taxing the colonists. But the colonists were not represented in England's **Parliament**. They felt this was unfair. The colonists began to talk of independence.

In 1774, New Hampshire patriots stole powder and guns from Fort William and Mary. The American Revolution began the next year. The colonists used the arms and powder to fight the English at the **Battle of Bunker Hill**.

On January 5, 1776, New Hampshire adopted its own **constitution**. Five months later, it was the first state to

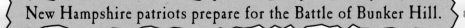
New Hampshire patriots prepare for the Battle of Bunker Hill.

declare independence from England. That same year, three New Hampshire men signed the **Declaration of Independence**. Colonists won their independence from England in 1783. They formed the United States of America.

In 1788, New Hampshire became the new nation's ninth state. New Hampshire's John Langdon was the first acting vice-president of the United States.

Today, manufacturing supports New Hampshire's **economy**. Also valuable to New Hampshire's economy are paper production, tourism, agriculture, and electronics.

TIMELINE

1603 - Martin Pring travels to New Hampshire area

1605 - Samuel de Champlain explores New Hampshire area

1614 - John Smith claims New Hampshire area for England

1620 - Council for New England formed

1621 - Council grants land to John Mason and Ferdinando Gorges

1623 - Pannaway Plantation founded; Dover Neck (Dover) founded

1630 - Pannaway Plantation abandoned; Strawbery Banke (Portsmouth) founded

1638 - Exeter founded

1639 - Hampton founded

1675 - King Philip's War

1679 - New Hampshire becomes a royal province

1689 - King William's War

1702 - Queen Anne's War

1741 - Benning Wentworth named first governor

1744 - King George's War

1754 - French and Indian War begins

1760 - England wins French and Indian War

1770 - Sir John Wentworth becomes governor

1774 - New Hampshire patriots raid Fort William and Mary

1776 - New Hampshire adopts its own constitution; declares independence from England

1783 - American Revolution ends; colonies gain independence

1788 - New Hampshire becomes a state

Glossary

Algonquian - a family of Native American languages spoken from Labrador, Canada, to the Carolinas and westward into the Great Plains.

Battle of Bunker Hill - June 17, 1775; a battle of the American Revolution, fought on Charlestown peninsula, which became a victory for the colonies.

bonnet - a cloth or straw hat tied under the chin and worn by women and children.

constitution - the laws that govern a state or country.

Declaration of Independence - an essay written at the Second Continental Congress in 1776, announcing the separation of the American colonies from England.

economy - the way a colony uses its money, goods, and natural resources.

fertilizer - something that, when added to the soil, helps plants grow.

militia - a group of citizens trained for war or emergencies.

mortar - a strong vessel in which a material is pounded.

Parliament - England's lawmaking group.

pestle - a club-shaped tool used to pound and crush something.

petticoat - a skirt worn beneath a dress.

province - one of the main divisions of a country.

Puritan - a member of a group of people who thought the Church of England needed some changes, but wanted to stay in it.

raid - a sudden attack.

stocks - a wooden device with holes to lock a person's head, hands, or feet in place and allow them to be publicly scorned.

tallow - the melted fat of cattle and sheep used in making candles and soap.

Web Sites

New Hampshire State Almanac
http://www.state.nh.us/nhinfo/history.html
This site has facts about New Hampshire's history and the state today.

Strawbery Banke Museum
http://www.strawberybanke.org
This is the site of a museum in Portsmouth, New Hampshire. It has pictures and information about historical homes, garrison houses, shops, and taverns.

These sites are subject to change. Go to your favorite search engine and type in New Hampshire Colony for more sites.

Index